Sometimes my child worries ... what do I do?

Sometimes my child worries ... what do I do?

The Support Book

A guide to understanding and managing children's anxiety. Use alongside 'Sometimes I worry ... how about you?'

Sometimes my child worries ... what do I do?

Published by Carina McEvoy

Editor: Elaine Collins
Cover Design: Lorraine Luby

The author of this book does not dispense medical advice or prescribe techniques as a form of treatment for any medical issue. The purpose of this publication is to act as an aide within the home or classroom.

ISBN 978-0-9935941-4-4

Acknowledgements

I would like to thank my family and friends for all the support they have shown me while writing this book, and the children's book, *Sometimes I worry ... how about you?* I also wish to thank my husband Brian for all his help and support. Without it these books would not have been written. He is my rock and my never-ending source of encouragement. Thank you also to June, a very special person who has given me so much inspiration throughout my life and to Demi, my unofficial life coach. I would like to extent my gratitude to Billy Arrigan who, since introducing me to Child Psychology, has provided so much advice during the writing of this book which can only be described as invaluable. And finally, to you the reader, I hope you find these books a source of empowerment for you and your child.

**To Anna and Ellie,
my greatest teachers in life!**

Foreword

We all know the state of the mental health services in this country and any help available to prevent our young people from reaching that stage where they need professional help and have become mired down in the quagmire of long waiting lists and overstretched services must be a positive thing.

Carina has compiled an innovative, relevant and badly needed set of aids and visual tools to help you and your children maintain a healthy level of mental health. These step-by-step pro-active strategies are based on the theories of Cognitive Behavioural Therapy, Neuro Linguistic Programming, Diaphragmatic breathing, Progressive Relaxation, Mantra and Mindfulness.

I would best describe it as a pre-emptive way for you to help your child deal with issues of stress and anxiety before it gets to a level where professional psychological help is needed. Prevention is always a better option than cure and these books and accompanying classes have what is needed to nip early signs of anxiety, stress and worry in the bud and give both you and your children a solid foundation on which to build and maintain a healthy level of mental health.

It is in-depth and comprehensive, but thoroughly researched and Carina lays it all out in clear and concise ways in which you can tackle these issues, and it is done in a child-friendly way, using child-appropriate language with easy to follow step-by-step guidelines. Carina shows you the way, but it is up to you to follow the path she clearly lays out, this is a process and it takes time and effort but if these books aid you in bringing up a child with good mental health then it must be worth the effort?

Billy Arrigan (BA, H-Dip in Further Education, Tutor in Child Psychology and Social Care)

Sometimes my child worries ... what do I do?

Contents:

Sometimes my child worries ... what do I do?

Sometimes my child worries ... what do I do?

Sometimes my child worries ... what do I do?

Quick technique finder:

Who wrote these two books about childhood anxiety?

A medical expert in the field of child psychology? No, but it was written by someone who has a lifetime's experience dealing first-hand with the effects of anxiety. Someone who has lived through it, felt it, fought it, lost against it, battled it again, gave into it, carried it around for years and finally got a handle on it.

My educational background consists of a Bachelor of Arts Degree in Sociology, Geography and Economics from The National University of Maynooth, the Higher Diploma in Education from University College Dublin and a Diploma plus Advanced Diploma in Hypnotherapy and Psychotherapy from ICC Cork. Most recently I have completed a QQI level six Child Psychology Course, a Practitioners' Certificate in Cognitive Behavioural Counselling and Neuro Linguistic Programming Practitioner Training. Up until my second child was born I worked as a teacher in secondary level education.

I am a strong believer in giving our children not only the coping skills to manage anxiety but also important life skills such as planning, problem solving and decision making along with the confidence they need to be resilient in today's world.

The resilience they develop as children will carry them throughout their adult life.

I have a genuine interest in mental health matters, more specifically in terms of anxiety and depression. I think that as adults, as parents, teachers, doctors, etc. we need to encourage good mental health within the generations following us.

In line with Donald W. Winnicott who became Britain's first medically-trained child psychoanalyst, I too believe that children are the very basis of our society. They are our future and it makes sense to look after them. I feel our society today is failing them. They need proper health care in terms of their mental health. Proper mental health education needs to become a priority within Government, filtering down to our medical services and our school system.

Reviewed by Professionals

I could not publish this book without first having it reviewed by professional therapists and experts who have experience in working with children and in the area of mental health.

Billy Arrigan

Child Psychology and Social Care Tutor

"Well-researched, innovative, relevant and timely. Going forward, I think this could be a real game changer in aiding our young children develop and maintain a good foundation for mental well-being."

Mari Gregan

Hypnotherapist/Psychotherapist

"The real importance of this book lies in demystifying anxiety for both the child and guardian. In child-friendly language, it describes what is happening in the flight or fight response for children. Which actually takes the mystery out of it and normalises it for children. That, in itself, gives the child the tools to be able to deal with their own feelings. How Mo, the anxious little creature, explains and supports the child through a set of 'tricks' empowers the child to help themselves. And being able to manage the anxiety by themselves gives both the child and the parent or guardian back that sense of control."

Sheila Haskins
Counsellor/Psychotherapist

"This child friendly approach to the whole area of anxiety is illustrated in a colourful, fun and easy to follow book aimed at young children. Parents and carers can sit with their young children and 'walk through' Mo's worries and fears and learn 'tricks' from Mo to assist the child. *Sometimes my child worries... what do I do?* explains in detail the knowledge needed to help their children along the way! As a teacher I welcome these books as an aid in assisting young children and parents/guardians alike to deal with anxiety."

Lyn Quigg
Primary School Teacher

"This child friendly approach to the whole area of anxiety is illustrated in a colourful, fun and easy to follow book aimed at young children. Parents and carers can sit with their young children and 'walk through' Mo's worries and fears and learn 'tricks' from Mo to assist the child. *Sometimes my child worries... what do I do?* explains in detail the knowledge needed to help their children along the way! As a teacher I welcome these books as an aid in assisting young children and parents/guardians alike to deal with anxiety."

What age child is this book best suited to?

The language and explanation of anxiety and the techniques used are appropriate from the age of five to approximately ten years old.

However, you know your child best and if it is suitable for their level of understanding. The techniques themselves can be used at any age, they are just laid out in a child friendly way.

A guide to using the children's book
(Sometimes I worry ... how about you?)

Sometimes I worry .... how about you? is a children's anxiety book that can be, and ideally should be, accompanied with *Sometimes my child worries ... what do I do? Support Book.*

They are purchased separately to allow for the child to keep the book with them without access to the adult content, which is not age appropriate. The support booklet offers greater insights into understanding and managing childhood anxiety. It also contains all the information needed to fully master the techniques used and explains why we use them.

What is in the children's book *Sometimes I worry ... how about you?*

✓ Age appropriate content
The book can be read with an adult or read alone depending on age of the child.

✓ Questions for the child
Questions lead to self-discovery and self-awareness. They also encourage discussion with an adult which in turn encourages the child to be open about what they are thinking and feeling.

✓ Creative spaces
Drawing and colouring, especially for the younger child, are great ways to relax and be calm and allow for expression of emotion. The older child may prefer to write in the boxes. The act of writing seems to tap into what our emotions really are. Journaling is a highly encouraged activity among the mental health profession as it is so beneficial for the recovery and maintenance of mental health.

✓ Resources
At the end of the child's book there are a number of resources/templates for the child to use.

✓ 17 techniques

Each technique is tailored to help the child reduce the level of anxiety experienced.

How to ensure best use of the children's book

No matter how old the child is, the adult should go through *Sometimes I worry ... how about you?* with them. This is particularly important when using the book for the first time to give that much-needed emotional and non-judgmental support.

It is important to commit to the child 100% while going through the book. Make sure you are reading it at a time when you can give your full level of patience, calmness, listening and encouragement. A relatively quiet and comfortable place is an ideal setting. Once the techniques are mastered they can be used anywhere, anytime and within a matter of minutes.

Will this book solve all the anxiety issues?

This book along with *Sometimes I worry ... how about you?* is designed to help both the adult and the child understand and manage child anxiety. Upon learning more about anxiety, the children's book teaches specific techniques to reduce anxiety levels. The techniques are taught in an age-appropriate and child-centred way. The aim is that children using the book will be able to carry out the techniques themselves. With time and practice, the dominance anxiety holds over the child's life may reduce significantly.

The techniques are a collection of powerful tools that you and your child can use. They are instant tools that can be used before, during and even after anxious events. They are simple pro-active strategies that will go a long way to relieve an anxious mind.

However, this course and these techniques are only one avenue of help and support available to you and your child. There is so much information available today surrounding mental health. If you think your child's anxiety is becoming a serious issue, then it could be time to think about seeking professional help.

Being vigilant about our children's mental health

We are encouraged to take care of our children's physical health. Babies and children are vaccinated against an array of illnesses. We have no problem giving our children vitamins or bringing them to A&E when necessary. We look after our children's dental health, teaching them to brush their teeth and making sure they do it twice daily. We now need to learn to look after their mental health because every child has mental health just as they have physical health and dental health. Mental health is so important and with all of today's stresses and strains it is vital to take time out to look after ourselves and our children. It is so important to know the signs of anxiety and to be able to read our children's mental health. Poor mental and emotional health is a very real issue.

Logic and reason go out the window when anxiety and depression take hold. There is no such thing as thinking straight. Sometimes people may not even realise that they are ill and therefore do not seek help. Children and young people especially may not know they are unwell. As educators, parents, guardians, doctors, etc. it is not only important to understand the basic signs and symptoms of poor mental health, but it is time we became as vigilant about it as we are about physical health.

Are we making too much out of child anxiety?

No! Our children are living in a world that has completely changed in the last generation and is totally different to their grandparents' childhood. They have access to all sorts of things that our grandparents never had and they do not have the same physical work demanded of them. We have machines for everything now and what might have been grown in our grandparents' garden can now be thrown into a trolley in the supermarket.
But look how the world has changed in other ways. The world can be a scary place to live in and it's all around us 24/7 on our radios, TVs, laptops and phones.

Our 'food' has changed so much. Can we even be sure what exactly is in the food that we are serving to our children? The amount of sugar added to our food and available to our children is a major cause for concern. Food is such an important aspect when it comes to mental health and balance is key. Helping our children become aware of the need for balance and develop their own sense of balance is also important. Simply restricting something can make it more appealing.

How we use our time has also changed. We are always in a rush. "Come on! Hurry! Quickly!" It is all go, go, go. We need to slow down. Practise being calm. Take time to catch up with each other and that means with the children, too. We need to be comfortable with doing nothing. With all the activities our children do these days, there is no time to experience boredom.

Which brings me to Low Tolerance Frustration, a key factor in anxiety. We have developed a Low Tolerance Frustration to boredom and to waiting. Children hate to be bored now. They spend so much time on their screens being entertained that they have lost the ability to entertain themselves. Children need to be able to use their imaginations: they need to be able to play! It is good for children to feel bored. That is when their creativity has a chance to shine. Screen time for children these days far outweighs simple playtime, reading or even simply running around outside in the fresh air! Balance is key.

Children also have a Low Tolerance Frustration to waiting as do many or us adults. We are so used to everything on demand in today's world. Google answers all our queries there and then. We can watch news anywhere at anytime. There is no such thing as waiting to sit down and watch the evening news anymore! Children can watch cartoons at any time of the day or night. Not that long ago you could switch on the TV but programming had ended for the day. Not that long ago we had to sit through all the ads. Now everything is instant and constant. Waiting is an anxious time for people these days. We cannot seem to stand it anymore. We have no tolerance for it and neither do our children. "Are we there yet? Are we there yet?"

Our idea of 'family' has changed over the years and families are changing all the time. And the bigger changes are on the increase. Divorce, separation, merging step-families, and parents working longer hours all have an impact on children. A dramatic change to a family situation means that children experience a time of re-adjustment to their new family life.

The bottom line is there is an epidemic of poor mental health among our children today compared to children growing up less than thirty years ago. We have to roll up our sleeves and do something about this. By simply even reading this book, you could be part of the solution.

Modelling Behaviour

One of our responsibilities as parents is to look at ourselves!

- Are we anxious?
- Are we negative?
- Are we stressed out?

Sometimes my child worries ... what do I do?

- Do we have a sense of competency in ourselves to manage life's hiccups?

- Do we freak out when our child climbs up onto the kitchen counter?

- Are we stuck with our heads in our phones all the time?

- Are we able to approach difficult situations with an air of calm?
- Do we face the world with fear and reluctancy?

- Do we have the important skills of planning and problem solving?

- Are we constantly running around with no time to sit down?

- Are we forgetting about the little things in life?

- When was the last time we listened (actually, fully and actively listened) to our children?

The first ever English Children's Medical Psychoanalyst Donald W. Winnicott (1896 – 1971) put forward the theory of the **Good Enough Mother.** According to Winnicott, what children need are parents who are good enough, not perfect! Good enough as ordinary, loving, supportive and empathetic parents.

In our quest to do the absolute best we can to make life perfect for our children and do we sometimes forget to sit down and actually just be good enough?

Are we constantly running around, run ragged, stressed and, busy, busy, busy? Do we fret about getting the washing done, the uniforms organised, the lunches made, the football kit dry, the money earned and the mortgage paid leaving little to zero energy left to properly look after ourselves let alone our loved ones?

Or are we the how-do-they-do-it-all parent with everything in their life completely under control? Every cushion in its place, the floor so clean you are afraid to walk on it, the children's homework edited to perfection? A parent who looks so in control from the outside, even intimidating. Could we be a bit like this?

Whatever way we behave, our children see it! They see our behaviour and they model it.

Do you recognise yourself here?

Sometimes my child worries ... what do I do?

How you can stop the cycle:

- Recognise it!
- Accept that you are doing your best.
- Get to know yourself and what pushes your buttons. What are your triggers? Awareness can be powerful.
- Be willing to look at your way of doing things and be willing to work at making the changes you need to make.
- Devise a plan for yourself as to how you are going to deal with the triggers.
- Use Cognitive Behavioural Therapy (CBT)/Neuro Linguistic Programming (NLP)/mindfulness, etc. on yourself.
- Listen to your children! Mindfully listening to your children is a tonic and it creates a bond. Children are funny, creative, inquisitive, wonderful little people so make sure you do not miss out on what they have to share.
- Know when you need time out for yourself.
- Realise if you have overreacted. Explain to your children why you overreacted and

discuss how you could have reacted in a more helpful way. Show your children how to retrace your steps and problem solve the situation to achieve a better end result.

- Seek support from family and friends.
- Seek support from a professional if you think you need that extra level of support.

Dealing with feelings at a young age

It is good that we teach our little ones how to deal with their feelings and their worries from a young age. Knowing how we feel, why we feel it and being comfortable about it is so important.

Far too often in this society we are uncomfortable with feelings. Men especially struggle with being able to show their feelings. It is important we, society that is, let our all our children feel their emotions and be comfortable with them.

Knowing what we are feeling is very important and very young children can become very frustrated because they simply do not know what it is they are feeling. It is good to be able to tell them. "You feel angry with Dad because you are not allowed have that bag of sweets and it is okay to be angry. But you are still not getting the sweets!"

Once children begin to understand their feelings they can begin to accept them and become comfortable with them. They become comfortable with themselves and can trust themselves and how they feel.

Adolescents tend to internalise their feelings so if we can help children become comfortable with their feelings and talking about them before that happens then great!

Talking to your child about anxiety

Anxiety is fast becoming an epidemic among our children. We shouldn't keep them sheltered from conversations about mental health even though we may feel sometimes that it is the right thing to do. They need to be aware of mental health just as they are aware of physical health.

Discussing mental health with our children openly and honestly will not only make them feel at ease talking about their feelings and their concerns but it will help end the stigma associated with mental health issues.

How to approach the subject of anxiety and mental health:

- ✓ Keep in mind that mental health is just the same as physical health. We all have mental health because we all have brains and minds. It is not something to afraid of. Do not be afraid to approach the subject.

- ✓ Be open and honest about mental health. This approach will make the child feel comfortable discussing it with you and it will encourage them to talk to you when they need to.

- ✓ Use age appropriate language. Be aware that as they grow, the nature of your child's questions and the detail and language of your answers will develop.

- ✓ Use everyday examples to discuss mental health. Refer to issues reported on TV, radio and in the paper.

- ✓ Talk to children about their feelings. Help them understand their feelings and show/teach them how to manage feelings in a healthy way.

- ✓ Find the best way that works for you to chat to your child. Casual conversations over a colouring book can sometimes be a great way to have a chat about certain issues. Older children talk better when they feel like they do not have to talk. So, combining it with an activity is good. Chatting while on a drive or while having a kick-about are also great opportunities to talk about certain issues.

Talking about anxiety specifically:

The best thing to do if your child has anxiety is think, **LEES:**

Label

Explain

Empathise

Strategise

LEES

- ✓ **Label** in an age-appropriate manner what the child is feeling.

- ✓ **Explain** anxiety to the child. Use language they will understand. Teach them all about anxiety and what it is useful for. Let the child know it's okay to feel anxious. Let the child know they have a really clever brain that is just being a little overprotective.

- ✓ **Empathise** with the child. We all know what it is like to feel anxious. Telling them not to worry or not to be silly isn't going to make the anxiety magically disappear. It will probably only make them more reluctant to come to you the next time they feel anxious.

- ✓ **Strategise** with the child. Teach some calming strategies to reduce the anxiety. Teach the child life strategies to help them deal with situations so that the anxiety may not even become an issue in the first place. These can be skills such as planning, problem solving and decision making. Build their self-confidence and resilience. Use the techniques in the children's book to help reduce anxiety.

Age-appropriate language in the children's book

It is in our children's best interests to speak to them about their anxieties and mental health. Being open and honest with them encourages them to talk to you about their anxiety, free from stigma. However, it is important to communicate with your child in an age-appropriate and child-friendly way.

In the children's book *Sometimes I worry ... how about you?* the word 'worry' is used instead of 'anxiety' and 'trick' is used instead of 'technique'. However, you know your child best and their ability to understand such terms. Use the words, terms and concepts that you feel your child is able for and comfortable with.

Tackling child anxiety without tackling confidence

What we say to and in front of our children is really important. They are like little sponges soaking up every single one of our words. We need to tackle their anxiety issues without impacting negatively on what they believe. There is no point in telling a child not to worry because they will anyway. You do not want them to think there is something seriously wrong with them because they worry. Or worse, you do not want them to feel that they cannot come to you with their worries. You need the child to know they can come to you about anything that bothers them. It can be very scary for a child if they think they have no one to turn to. Simply listening to the child explain what is on their mind is comforting to them. Sometimes, a calm and patient ear is all a child needs.

It is important also that we do not put the child down in any way for being worried about something, even if it is ridiculous to us. Especially if we are tired after a long day and our patience is decreasing fast. For example, do not say "Don't be silly!" to the child that is worrying about a monster lurking under the bed. It may seem silly to you but to them, it is far from silly. It is a real fear, a real worry and telling the child that he or she is silly to be feeling that way, only makes them feel worse. Accept that their worry is real for them.

Sometimes my child worries ... what do I do?

Supporting children through their worries is important. Help them deal with it by giving them the tools they need to overcome the worry. Explain to them why they do not need to worry about it. The solution could be as simple as a two-minute conversation!

Cognitive Behavioural Therapy works brilliantly for tackling anxious thoughts in a positive and helpful way. Whatever way we choose to talk to our children about their worries, it is so important that in doing so we leave their confidence intact.

Example:

Compare the following reaction to the child that is crying because there are monsters under her bed:

1. "Okay, so you think there are monsters under your bed. I'll have a look .... Nope, no monsters there. But I know where they are; they are actually in your imagination because you have a really good imagination. Wow, look at what you imagined. I bet you can imagine an elephant, too. What colour is your elephant? Wow, you imagined a big grey elephant! Haven't you got a brilliant imagination? Well, that's exactly where your monster is coming from. And guess who is in charge of your imagination?

Yes, you are! That's right, well done! So, you can tell your imagination what you want to think about. Let's think about some lovely horses galloping along the sea, what colour will they be? Do you want to imagine yourself riding one of them and splashing into the water? Imagine if they had wings and you flew into the sky and through the clouds…"

2. "Monsters under your bed? Don't be silly; there are no such things!"

The first scenario leaves the child feeling good about their imagination and has a sense of being able to deal with the worry of the monster whereas scenario two just leaves the child feeling silly and over time they may even stop telling you about their fear or worry at all. That is something we should avoid. The most important thing for our kids is that they feel comfortable talking to us about what they are thinking and/or feeling.

Confidence Building

There are so many ways we can challenge our children to gain more confidence. The following is only a few suggestions.

Everyday responsibilities – "You can do this!"

Expand and stretch their belief in themselves by giving them some responsibility. Learning that they CAN do it, is an important lesson.

That can mean something as simple as letting them pay for something they want in the shop, getting the change and interacting with the shopkeeper. Teach them to cook something simple or if they are too young, let them help prepare a meal.

Chores

Children thrive on age-appropriate jobs. It gives them confidence in their capabilities but it also teaches them about responsibility. Having confidence and a sense of responsibility makes life a bit easier as they are growing up and when they become adults themselves.

Clubs and sports

There are so many clubs and activities that children can be a part of to give their confidence a growth spurt. Swimming, ballet, football, Girl Guides, Scouts, surfing, taekwondo, gymnastics, horse riding, the list goes on and on. Even one activity a week can go a long way in developing their self-confidence and self-belief.

Exposure therapy

This is a behavioural therapy used to address certain anxieties. It is very useful with children's anxiety. It basically means exposing the child to the cause of their anxiety in tiny bite-size pieces, bit by bit, in order to decrease the anxiety felt each time.

Resilience Building

By reading this book and going through the children's book with the child, you are automatically building and nurturing the child's resilience. Anything that helps the child to deal with their anxiety in a positive way is resilience strengthening.

What is resilience?

Resilience is all about being about to bounce back from a difficult situation. Resilient children can face life with a good sense of curiosity, bravery and versatility.

Sun cream

The great thing about resilience is that it acts a bit like sun cream! You apply sun cream to your children before they go out on a sunny day. Why? To protect them from the sun's harmful rays so they don't damage their skin. When we apply sun cream, their skin will still get the sun. However, we have avoided the real pain of sunburn and lasting sun damage.

Resilience can be viewed in the same way. We should think of it as a *guard* against adversity in life. Building resilience in our children does not mean they will not meet difficult times. Just like the sun cream, they still get the sun! Sun cream doesn't ward off the sun. So, it is the same with resilience, being resilient does not mean we are warding off difficulties in life, because they will always face us. That is life. But by building resilience, like applying sun cream, we are preventing the ability of the difficult situation to have a painful and lasting negative effect on the child – emotionally and psychologically.

Resilience for life

Instilling resilience in the child now will help guard them through adolescence and adulthood.

Do not disturb!

This of course, is not to say that children and adults will not be distressed when 'bad things' happen. The aim of resilience building is to make sure that distress does not 'disturb' their living.

Resilience building strategies in the children's book:

- Creating a supportive bond.
- Promoting talk.
- Letting the child know it's okay to ask for help.
- Positive role modelling.
- Helpful language.
- Supportive and positive self talk.
- Helpful body language.
- Reframing negative to positive.
- Encouraging positivity.
- Believing in their capabilities.
- Allowing them time to rescue themselves.
- Using the power of the imagination for good.
- Mindfulness.
- Progressive relaxation.
- Emotional understanding of self.

- Confidence building.
- Exposure therapy.
- Mantra use.
- Problem solving skills.
- Planning skills.
- Decision making skills.
- Versatility.

The Imagination – Our secret weapon

Anxiety is future based. It is being anxious about something that has not even happened yet. The irrational thoughts that go through our heads are usually based on phrases like: What if such and such a thing happens? It must not happen! It would be the end of the world if it did happen! It would be so awful, I wouldn't be able to cope!

Have you ever noticed that our imagination can really run away with itself in these anxious moments? We can imagine the most awful scenarios possible. Children are no different. Their imagination causes their anxiety to spiral out of control.

However, the imagination is not the enemy here. In fact, it can actually be used as a secret weapon to guard against anxiety.

Sometimes my child worries ... what do I do?

It is helpful to teach our children that it is their imagination that is scaring them, thinking up all sorts of awful 'What ifs?'. But just as we spoke about tackling anxiety without tackling their confidence, it is equally as important to talk about their imagination with positivity. Make the child aware that it is their imagination that is coming up with these awful scenarios but that they can harness that same imagination and use it to think about something good, positive and happy.

Praise a child for their powerful imagination and make them understand just how good it is. They will begin to feel proud of their imagination when you talk about it with such positivity.

"Wow, that's some amazing imagination you have! Look what you managed to do ... you actually managed to frighten yourself so much that your heart is actually beating faster! That means your imagination is absolutely brilliant! You are really creative! I wonder what else you can imagine?"

The Imagination and deciding how to use it

Depending on the age of the child, it is a good idea to introduce 'choices' when it comes to using their imagination. Children love choices and being able to choose. Explain to the child that they have the *choice* to use their imagination to think about something scary and awful or to use it to think about something positive and more cheerful.

With younger children, set up some 'imagination' time for them. For example, when putting your child to bed, give them five shapes and ask them to make a picture in their mind using the shapes. Or create a picture for them and ask them to think about how they would colour it in.

The key idea here however, is that the imagination can play a key role in combating anxious thoughts.

A lot of the tricks used in this course will call on the role of the imagination!

The Power of Choice

From the age of two years old it is valuable to help a child develop the skill of making choices. We all want our children to be able to make good choices but let's not overlook the importance of even being able to make a choice.

From the age of two, children begin to see themselves as a separate identity. They begin to take control over their own body and what they want to play with and eat. 'No' becomes their favourite word as they try to exercise their new-found independence and to express their autonomy.

Sometimes my child worries ... what do I do?

A sense of balance is important at this stage as it is important to respect some of their 'no' decisions, because as teens then they will feel more confidence saying no to peer pressure. However, it is also important to set healthy boundaries.

Why it is good to give children choices:

- Making choices is a life skill that has to be learned. This skill makes life so much easier when they are older.
- Children feel they have some control over what they do.
- Leads to better behaviour. Children feel respected and the battle of wills is often forgotten about.
- Encourages independence and self-reliance.
- Promotes confidence in their ability to decide.
- They will appreciate a choice more so than a demand or command.

Giving choices to children:

- Give choices you can agree to.
- Give choices that are age appropriate to them. What story they want going to bed? What they would like for breakfast: eggs or cereal? What shoe do they want to put on first?
- Let them decide and be okay with whatever option they choose.

Making good choices:

- Model good choices. Say what your options are, what you choose and why. E.g "I can have brown bread or a bag of crisps for lunch. I think I'll have the brown bread because it is healthier."
- Talk through the pros and cons of each option, then let them decide.
- Allow them to make a poor choice as this is also an important learning experience. Let them learn from your poor choices also (if they are appropriate).

The exercise, water, food and mood link

H2O for a healthy mind flow!

We all know the importance of drinking water; without it we get dehydrated. Dehydration leads to a lack of concentration, tiredness, fatigue, poor mental performance among other physical issues. Children need to keep hydrated by drinking 6-8 glasses of water/milk/fruit/vegetable juice a day.

Exercise for a mood rise!

Exercise is undeniably good for us. Apart from all the obvious physical benefits, exercise also provides us with many mental health benefits. It actually enhances the brain's metabolism which results in better brain function. Children who exercise have better memory skills and can concentrate better in school. Exercise burns off excess harmful hormones while releasing hormones such as endorphins and serotonin, the happy hormones, which greatly benefit the mind. Therefore, it isn't all that surprising that regular exercise decreases anxiety and depression.

A balanced diet to eat right!

Eating right is really important. We know that when we eat badly we feel bad, right? It is the same for our children. They need nutritious food to keep their bodies, brains and minds healthy. As with everything in life, we need a healthy balance. It is important to sustain our bodies with nutritional food but also to enjoy something for our sweeter tooth within the healthy guidelines!

Explaining the importance of good nutrition to your child

Explain nutrition to the child using concepts they understand.

Example:

"Think of a car. A car gets us from *a* to *b*. Our body is like a car; it gets us from *a* to *b*. A car needs clean water to clean the windscreen. It needs clean oil and clean petrol or diesel. If you put dirty water, oil or fuel into the car, it will not work as well and will probably even break down. Your body is the same. It needs clean, nutritious food to keep your body working well."

Tools and techniques taught in the children's book

The techniques used are based on the following therapies:

- Deep diaphragmatic breathing
- Mindfulness
- Progressive relaxation
- Mantra use
- Cognitive Behavioural Therapy (CBT)
- Neuro Linguistic Programming (NLP)

These are all beneficial therapies which would be so valuable within the primary school curriculum. Parents/guardians should familiarise themselves with the basics as everyone experiences anxiety on some level. The techniques in this book are simple to follow and show children the power we have over own own thoughts, feelings and behaviour which promotes physical, emotional and mental well-being.

Notes and Techniques Section

This section corresponds with the children's book *Sometimes I worry...how about you?*

The children's book is written from the perspective of Mo, a cute little anxious creature who tells the child in his childlike way all about his worries and how he deals with them.

In this section, each underlined heading and trick in the children's book is further detailed for your information here.

Please note that the tricks (techniques) headings are in italics in the children's version. They are laid out in a bullet point format, as a step-by-step guide on how to carry out the technique.

Worrying is all very natural

Anxiety is a natural response to the threat of endangerment or even death. Going back to cavemen style thinking, endangerment of lives was the reality every day. Hunting for food alone was a serious dangerous activity. The science behind anxiety is actually very interesting. Basically our brain kicks into flight or fight mode. This is explained fully in the tricks section with trick number one.

Sometimes my child worries ... what do I do?

The thing to remember is that anxiety is actually a mechanism that keeps us safe. The problem with anxiety arises however when it is a response given to a situation that does not warrant it. Our brain is kicking into this flight or fight mode without the actual danger being present. We have crossed over from a natural worry or concern to anxiety. We are reacting to irrational thoughts in our heads. We all have irrational thoughts in our heads. There is simply no escape from forming them as we grow and are moulded by our environment and by society.

So anxiety is a great response should our safety depend on it but more and more people are feeling anxious when the threat is not there. This anxiety is actually rendering us powerless, making us feel like we have no control over situations and no ability to make rash choices. Is it irrational and ineffective?

Why is it natural to worry?

To explain why it is natural to worry we need to look at the Flight or Fight Response.

The Flight or Fight Response

Walter Cannon, an American physiologist first came up with this model in the 1920s. It explains what happens to the body when faced with danger. If a person faces endangerment, they respond either by:

Fight

Stay and fight the danger in order to survive.

or

Flight

Flee the situation in order to survive.

Both responses require the body and mind to be able to cope to the best of its ability to ensure safety/survival.

Biologically the body experiences a flood of changes to the hormones and neurotransmitters to help prepare the body for action.

Some of the changes that occur are:

- Chemicals such as adrenaline and cortisol are released into the bloodstream.
- The increase of chemicals raises the respiratory rate.
- Blood flow is directed to the limbs for fast moving action.
- Blood flow is also directed to the muscles for quick and strong movement.

- Pupils dilate and sight becomes sharpened.
- Awareness of surroundings is heightened.

So, if you were to come across a lion chasing towards you licking his lips, would you not want your natural Flight or Fight Response to kick in?

Anxiety, when taking Cannon's Flight or Fight into consideration is not only natural but necessary. The problem with anxiety is when it is experienced without the danger present.

Our thoughts/Our feelings

Quite simply, our thoughts and feelings are connected. If our thoughts are negative, we feel negative. If we feel negative, we think negatively. If our thoughts are positive, we feel positive. And if we feel positive, we think positively.

A lot of the techniques used in the children's book work on changing the thought. If we can change the thought, then we can change the feeling.

Getting the child to label the feeling

One of the most frustrating things for children is that they do not know how to express what it is they are feeling. They want to tell the adult so the adult will understand but they do not know how to do that.

Sometimes my child worries ... what do I do?

Sometimes, they may not know how they are actually feeling at all. This can be very unsettling for children.

Even adults can feel unsettled when we think we are not understood or if our feelings are not taken into consideration, especially by those closest to us, it can be frustrating and hurtful.

It is good to help children understand how they feel. And it is vital that they know that whatever feeling they have, *it is okay*. It is how they react to the feeling that is important.

There are safe and appropriate responses to our feelings. Being able to talk through our feelings in a safe, non-judgmental environment is always a good place to start.

For younger children, it is good to help them label how they feel. For example, "You feel sad because you lost Teddy? It's okay to feel sad. It's okay to cry."

Crying is a normal and healthy response to feeling sad or hurt. We should never mock or make children feel silly for crying for a legitimate reason.

Changing our thoughts

If we know that a negative thought will bring about a negative feeling, then we know it is logical to change that negative thought.

Sounds easy. But thinking in a negative pattern is almost like a habit that we need to break. And we can only do that with time, practice and a lot of patience.

The technique *'How thoughts can be positive'* is a way of breaking this habit but it really needs to be practised as much as possible. Any time you hear your child speaking negatively about a situation/event/themselves, etc, use this technique to challenge their negativity.

Beware of your own thinking patterns however. This goes back to modelling behaviour. Be aware of where your child is picking up these thinking habits and patterns.

The following is a list of really common negative thinking patterns. See if you fall into any of the patterns on the list. If you do, or if you tend to think negatively, then use this technique to change your own way of thinking.

Sometimes my child worries ... what do I do?

Negative thinking patterns we fall into:

Negative thinking pattern	Kind of things we say....
All or nothing	"It has to be absolutely perfect or else it's no good."
Catastrophising	"That will be the worst thing ever!"
Overgeneralising	"That went really badly so I'm sure everything else will now too."
Mind reading	"They never rang me back, it's because they don't like me!"
Fortune telling	"I'll definitely fail that exam."
Personalisation	"I bet that's because of me, I didn't do it right."
Minimalising	"I got an A on that test but the questions were really easy so I'm sure everyone got the same."
Should statements	"I should get that done/ they should have called me/they should have invited me, too."
Mental filtering – only allowing the negatives in	"Nothing ever goes right for me."

Technique 1 – How thoughts can be positive

This is a technique based on the Cognitive Behavioural Therapy premise that it is not the situation that causes us upset, it is how we think about the situation. Therefore, with Cognitive Behavioural Therapy we work on changing the unhelpful negative thought. This is a very simple technique to teach the child to be aware of how they are thinking and to change their negative thinking to something more positive. It is a technique that will improve over time as the child becomes more skilled at thinking about the situation with a more positive frame of mind. It is a good technique for the child to learn as it reminds them of the power they have to change their thoughts. This technique is for everyday use, from the smallest negative thought to the biggest. With time and daily practice, it will help the child avoid those negative and anxious thinking patterns.

"But … I don't know why I feel …" ☹

Children are pretty good at pinpointing the situation or reason why they developed the thought in the first place. It is only when we grow older that we lose the reason for the thought. There'll be more on this idea later. Sometimes children do not know why they feel this way, but they *do know* the thoughts they are thinking. It may just be a little muddled and need a little unravelling.

The best thing to do when a child says he/she does not know why they are feeling worried or anxious about something is to *remain calm and ask what thoughts are in their head.* What is going through their mind? What thoughts are they listening to and thinking about?

For example, say to the child, "When you think about going to school, you get worried. So, what thoughts are in your head when you think about going to school? What things are you thinking about? What does that little voice in your head say?"
Reassure the child that we all have that little voice – self-talk. Continue the process of asking, "What thoughts are in your head when you feel…? etc. until you crack the culprit thought.

Most thoughts that bring about anxiety are simply unhealthy thoughts blown out of proportion, even if they stem from a genuine, real situation.

For example, "I can't read out my English homework, everyone will laugh at me and think I am the most stupid person in school!"

In this example, the issue of reading may be a real issue for the child, they may be scared to read aloud. But the thought that everyone will laugh at them and think that they are 'the most stupid person in the world' is a product of their anxious, negative self talk. They are imagining this nightmare scenario but it seems pretty real to them. We want to challenge the unhelpful thoughts and help the child to tackle similar thought processes the next time an issue arises for them. The techniques in this book are some ways these thoughts can be challenged. The child may have a genuine problem with reading but once the anxiety is under control, you can work on the reading.

Changing the thought before it becomes too stubborn to change!

As adults, unhelpful thoughts are built into our subconscious time and time again. We absorb them through our environment, our culture, our family, our experiences, etc. We then spend years going around in this vicious circle of thoughts, feelings, sensations and behaviour. The more time we give them, the more cemented the thoughts become. They become part of who we are and what we believe. The feelings we associate with those thoughts stay with us and the thought becomes so powerful it is hard to change.

In children, however, the timeframe for the 'thought' to cement into a hard-core belief is less! That is good news! If we can challenge the thought, the child will be less likely to grow up believing it and it won't become a lifelong issue to deal with.

Self talk

Everyone engages in self talk – that little voice in our heads. However, we own that voice and we are in complete control of what that voice says to us.

However, for people and indeed children dealing with strong negative emotions such as anxiety, that voice can feel like it is controlling us in a negative, harsh and unsympathetic way.

Children need to be encouraged to engage in positive self talk. The kind of talk they would use when speaking to a friend. Kind and positive self talk may feel strange at first. Even for a child, it is so much easier to berate yourself than compliment yourself. However, with time and practice, it can become easier to use a more positive tone.

Feeling the feelings in our bodies

Feelings are felt in our body. The sensations that hunger, thirst, heat and cold give us are felt in our body. However, the kind of feelings we are talking about here are feelings that we feel in our body and in our minds i.e. our emotions. Our emotions can have such a powerful effect over our physical body. The sensations they give us are our bodies' way of reacting to them.

Sometimes my child worries ... what do I do?

Think about when we are angry. We feel it in our mind but at times anger can make us breathe faster, go red in the face, shake, etc. Hurt can give us that lump in our throat. Anxiety gives us so many sensations: butterflies in our tummy, heart racing, breathing faster, sweaty hands, etc.

It is good for you to know how the child experiences the physical symptoms of anxiety. These body sensations may give you a clue as to how the child is feeling if they complain about certain aches and pains. A belly ache may not be a bug or a pain, it may be anxiety. When using the child's book, *Sometimes I worry ... how about you?* ask the child to scan their own body for these sensations. Recognising what the sensation is extremely helpful and can calm the child who otherwise may feel there is something wrong with them physically. It also gives you, the adult, the information you need to deal with the child's symptoms appropriately i.e. is the child sick or anxious?

Prolonged negative emotions can ultimately cause other illness so it is important that we deal with our feelings and emotions and do not carry them with us through life.

Do you ever feel nervous?

Being nervous is natural. We need to let the child know that it's okay to feel nervous but it is good to push through the nervousness. And, once you have done something for the first time over with, handled that difficult situation or met that new person, etc. then the nerves will settle down. Our nerves are just protecting us from the unknown, from the unfamiliar situation.

Technique 2 – Tell your body that it's okay!

This is a simple yet powerful technique whereby the child uses their self talk for reassurance and to encourage themselves to push through the nervousness. The act of acknowledging how you feel and why you feel that way helps lessen the sensation. It also puts a positive spin on feeling nervous. Remind the child that being nervous is a good thing and that their nerves are protecting them from an unknown situation or a situation they are uncomfortable with. Thanking their nerves for protecting them and telling themselves that they will be okay, affirms their confidence in their ability to deal with the situation. This can be a very powerful act.

Technique 3 – Turning nervousness into excitement

With this technique we are simply switching the word 'nervousness' for a more positive word: excitement. The sensations we feel are the same for both nervousness and excitement. With this technique, the child is asked to recall a memory of a time when they felt really excited about something. They then try to reframe their present nervousness with that feeling of excitement.
The aim is to relate the sensations to something positive rather than negative. When we focus on the positive, our attitude automatically shifts to one of confidence and resilience

Using our Imaginations

Our imaginations are extremely powerful tools to use in the eradication of, and recovery from, anxiety and depression. The techniques used in the children's book all seek to harness the power of the imagination.

Some people can see images very clearly in their imaginations. But if you or the child you are working with can't, don't fret! A clear, distinct image isn't always necessary. Some people can *sense* what it is they are imagining while others can conjure up *sounds* easily.

Answer this:

What is your favourite food in the entire world? What does it look like? When did you last eat it? What did it taste like? What does it smell like? What is it you like about it?

I bet in some way you sensed the food you were thinking of. Did you see it in your mind? Remember the taste of it? Remember the smell of it? Could you hear it sizzle, cook, pop, being poured? Could you remember the texture of it on your tongue or even on your fingertips? Well, that was your imagination at work and it sometimes even has the power to make you salivate!

"Relaxation is key where imagination is required."

Where the imagination is used in a technique, it is important that the child has a quiet and calm place to carry out the technique. The more relaxed the child is, the better the technique will work. At the beginning of each technique, where they need to close their eyes and conjure up an image, ask the child to take some long, slow, deep breaths to bring about a greater feeling of relaxation. The 4/4/4 breathing (the blow up a balloon trick) is an ideal way to start any technique.

Can you breathe from your belly?

When we are anxious we tend to breathe from the chest which causes the imbalance of the oxygen and carbon dioxide levels in the body. A lot of people automatically breathe from the chest all of the time from the result of simply becoming used to it that way.
Animals and new born babies automatically breathe from their bellies, their diaphragm to be precise. Most people breathe from their diaphragm while asleep. Breathing from the diaphragm relaxes the body and mind.

Technique 4 – Blow up a balloon in your tummy

This technique is a very easy way to teach the child to breathe from their belly. It is basically a method of taking long, slow, deep breaths and then exhaling slowly.

It is also a good way of calming a distressed mind as we are asking the child to focus on the balloon in their tummy rather than on their breathing. When a child is highly anxious, they may not feel like they are able to breathe at all. The 'balloon' is used as a distraction while they are actively stabilising their breathing.

This technique also prompts relaxation and is an ideal start to any meditation. The image of the balloon helps the child focus on their breathing and it is a great way to help them concentrate on the task.

Technique 5 – Replacing the yucky in my tummy

This technique reframes the negative as a positive. It is important to remember to replace the negativity with positivity and not leave a void. It is a really effective technique to use and, although it may sound complicated, it is a very easy technique to work through. The visualisation the child is asked to do strengthens the result of the technique. Visualising the shapes, colours, etc. makes the sensations seem tangible and easier to control. This cements the positive impact of the process for the person. The child is asked to use their belly breathing (diaphragmatic breathing) and imagination here so remember to go somewhere comfy and quiet. Children are great at visualising and generally accept this type of exercise more readily than adults. They tend to believe what they are visualising.

Technique 6 – The 'What then?' game

This technique involves bringing the child right through their problem or anxious situation and asking them 'what then?' until they conclude that ultimately the outcome will be okay. Give the child the time and space to really think through the issue logically. Depending on their age, you may need to prompt an answer. For example, "Do you think you would …?"/"I wonder would such and such a thing happen …"

It is important however, that the child stays realistic and doesn't dramatise (catastrophise) their answers to the "What then?" questions.

This is a great technique for anyone to use and it can be carried out anywhere at any time. It is a technique that works on changing that negative thought pattern of making a big deal out of little things. With practice it gets easier for the child to conclude, "It will all be okay, I suppose."

Technique 7 – Standing like a superhero

Body language not only tells other people how to read our mood, it also tells our own mind. In this technique, the child is asked to conjure up the image of their favourite superhero and to adopt the body language of that superhero. Guide them to a courageous and confident superhero if they are having difficulty thinking of one! Depending on the superhero they choose…. will be one of courage and confidence. By changing their posture to one of confidence, they will also feel an element confidence within their body and mind. Body language can 'trick' our minds into a more positive and confident feeling.

Technique 8 – My poem

Mo's poem, which will be turned into the child's poem, is another tool they can use when they feel anxious. Encourage the child to say this poem to themselves during times when they begin to feel anxious. Over time, the words will become lodged into the child's mind and resonate with the mind positively. During times of distress the words will bring a sense of calm.

The poem technique is based on the idea of the mantra. A mantra is a statement that, when repeated enough times (usually to yourself), can embed itself into the belief system.

Mantras are believed to have been first used within Hinduism as far back as 3000 years ago. Today however, mantras are used by many people and believed to have extremely positive psychological effects. Of course, the use of repetitive statements or words was, and still is, a common practice among many religions and cultures.

Technique 9 – Using a silly voice!

This technique works best when the child can carry it out in a calm and quiet place and in a relaxed manner. Ensure the child is comfortable. Start off this technique with a few deep breaths to help the child become more fully relaxed and able to give their full attention and concentration to their imaginary 'worry'. Then slowly work through the technique.

Technique 10 – Squeeze and let go

We all carry stress and tension in our muscles and that can lead to physical pain. The flight or fight response plays havoc with our muscles as they are ready for action; yet no action happens. When children are stressed and anxious, they too can feel this tension without realising it. This technique of progressive relaxation is a really soothing meditation to carry out with the child. Using your guiding voice, talk the child through the actions. The child will become progressively more relaxed as they squeeze and relax the muscles in their body, from their head to their toes. Initially, this technique is nicer when someone is talking you through it, but the child can learn to use self talk to use this technique alone.

Not really my worries!

Sometimes children pick up snippets of grown-up conversations or information on the news and feel the weight of the world on their shoulders. Some children worry about their parents as much as their parents worry about them. They also worry about things that are beyond their years or are simply not their job to worry about.

It is important that the child understands the 'worry' is not theirs and that their parent/guardian/teacher is fully capable of dealing with the 'worry' whatever it may be.

We are not teaching the child not to care about or be considerate to others nor are we shielding them from reality. We are simply taking away their need to worry about grown-up issues. It is our job as adults, parents, guardians, teachers, etc, to help them understand what is, or more to the point, what is NOT their worry to take on.

Modelling behaviour of course is also important here as the child looks to the adult on how to approach and handle issues. If we sweat the small stuff; they'll do the same.

Technique 11 – How to give your worries to a grown-up

This technique is a simple active representation of giving the worry away. The child will feel that they have actively given the worry to the adult and therefore more will be more likely to drop the worry from their own mind.

Technique 12 – My worry envelope for stubborn worries

This is a simple way of getting the child to 'let go' of their worries for a while. It is a great technique for anybody to use and works very well. It is a way of parking the worry. While the worry is in the envelope, encourage the child to say the rhyme:

"The worry is in the envelope, it is safe there.
Until I take it out again, for that worry I won't care."

While the poem should be easy for the child to remember, please note that younger children may need help recalling the rhyme!

When that particular worry crops up in their head again they will automatically think, "Oh yeah, I put that worry away for the moment, so I needn't worry about it right now."

Some concerns will need to be dealt with so taking them back out of the envelope when the time is right and the child is ready may be necessary. However, the child may realise it was a worry they didn't need to carry around or that putting it aside made them realise they want to let go of the worry altogether. It all depends on the nature of the worry.

Technique 13 – The casting a net trick

The aim is to get the child to a stage where they can use this technique on their own but in the beginning, it can very useful to guide them through this technique with a soft gentle voice. The more they practise, the better the technique will work. It is a simple way to help the child take the worry off their mind. They imagine taking it out of their head, shrinking and squashing it. Over time with practice, it should become a simple technique that they can use in any situation.

Worries can make you a brilliant time traveller!

Anxiety is future based, it is worrying about something that hasn't even happened. Here we try to help the child understand that there is no point worrying about the future. However, with an emotion as strong as anxiety, it can be hard for the child to take that on board. Therefore, it is good to be able to plan for anxious moments as much as you can.

Helping the child become good at problem solving is another way to alleviate some of that anxiety. The next two techniques focus on planning and problem solving.

Technique 14 – My plan

Anxiety is something that can make us feel that we have no control, that we'd have no way of coping with an anxious situation if it were to happen. The awfulness of it would seem like the end of the world. With thoughts like these, anxiety has control over the person.

Planning for events or anxious moments in life is just a simple way of putting mechanisms in place to make life easier for ourselves. It gives people back that sense of control. Putting a plan in place puts people at ease and can reduce all the brain noise or brain fog that can be felt when we are stressed out and anxious. Having a plan takes the anxiety out of the situation

Planning is like a having a fire escape plan in place.

Having a plan in place for when a fire breaks out reduces the panic in such a situation. If a fire were to occur, everyone knows what to do, where to go and to stay calm. If there was no fire escape plan in place, imagine the pandemonium if a fire ever broke out. It is the same with anxiety. If we know an event is likely to trigger anxiety, it is important for us to have an anxiety escape plan that we can carry out in a calm way.

In terms of children's anxiety, it is important to teach the skill of planning for events/situations in life that could trigger anxiety. If children have an anxiety escape plan in place, the situation will be less overwhelming and more manageable.

Planning Strategies

1. Discuss with your child what it is they are worried about.

2. Listen to their concerns without judging them as 'silly'. Remember, our imaginations make things real to us no matter how silly they may seem to others.

3. For each concern, taking the biggest one first, create a plan of action for the eventuality of it happening. Let the child think of their own ideas for the plan of action to develop valuable thinking and problem-solving skills.

4. Go over the plan with your child and make sure they are happy with it and feel less anxious.

5. Make sure you let them know you have complete belief in them being able to deal with the situation.

Example:

Your child is going on their first ever sleepover but they are anxious about it.

1. *Discuss with your child what it is they are worried about:*
   "What if I wake up and everyone is asleep, and I'm scared and want to come home?"

2. *Listen to their concerns without judging them as 'silly'. Remember, our imaginations make things real to us no matter how silly they may seem to others.*

3. *For each concern, taking the biggest one first, create a plan of action for the eventuality of it happening. Let the child think of their own ideas for the plan of action. They are using valuable thinking and problem-solving skills here.*

Plan of action:

- Bring teddy for comfort.
- We can talk to your friend's parents and tell them how you are feeling.
- We will ask them to check on you before they go to bed.
- If you wake up in the night you can call them.
- They will ring me, and I will collect you.

4. *Go over the plan with your child and make sure they are happy with it and it has lessened the anxiety felt.*

   "Okay this is the plan …. Are you happy with this plan? Do you think it will make you feel better going for the sleepover?

5. *Make sure you let them know you have complete belief in their being able to deal with the situation:*

   "You can deal with this! I know you can. No matter what happens, you are brave and able to deal with it!"

A Common Result

Chances are your child will be at ease with the notion of going on the sleepover now that there is a plan in place and they will have no issues at all! Knowing that they have planned ahead and that if X happens they have a plan of action to help them deal with it, will reduce their anxiety at the thought of X happening.

An Important Lesson

You are teaching your child that they can deal with the situations they fear. You are also relaying a very important message to them that you believe in them and their ability to deal with the situation and their own emotions. This in turn will increase their confidence levels in their own abilities.

Expect the Unexpected

The unexpected can throw a curveball in the wrong direction and set off all anxiety alarms but if children are taught how to plan for these moments, anxiety doesn't need to become a real issue. Find out/know what is likely to cause concern for your child. Put a plan in place for such situations.

Example:

If something comes up and you are ten minutes late collecting your child from school, have a plan in place so they will not be panicking at the school gate wondering why you are late and worrying about what has happened to you and what will happen to them. Other plans to put in place include plans for when the child gets lost, plans for when they are to perform on stage, etc.

Technique 15 – Working it out with the magic code

Problem solving skills are key life skills which children need to learn and practise. Once they have developed such skills, any future situation or issue that presents itself, that could potentially be an anxious time for the child, will become something they can easily work around.

To teach problem solving:

- ✓ Do not helicopter parent (hovering over and rushing in). Allow them to make mistakes and figure it out.
- ✓ Allow children to fail! Failure is a healthy to experience. It is also a learning experience. It is so important to encourage children to learn why something failed or didn't work out and

move on to another solution. Failure is simply feedback on what does or does not work. It is always a chance to learn.

- ✓ Ask your child for help. Practise problem solving in the home.

- ✓ Teach the 5-Step Problem Solving Process: **P**ercy **T**he **B**ear **P**lants **T**rees. This is detailed on the following page.

The 5-Step Problem Solving Process:

Percy The Bear Plants Trees

Word to remember	Letter	Stands for	Explanation
Percy	P	Problem	What is the *problem*? They talk; you listen. This may even be enough to help the situation.
The	T	Think	*Think* of a solution or a set of solutions to the problem. They can be good solutions or silly ones! Encourage the child to come up with others.
Bear	B	Best	Which is the *best* solution to use? Help the child to weigh up each solution and decide which is the best one to go with.
Plants	P	Pick	*Pick* a solution to use. Patiently guide the child to the best possible solution.
Trees	T	Try	*Try* out the solution. If it works, great! If it doesn't, then try another one.

The 'magic' code Percy The Bear Plants Trees is a mnemonic to help the child remember the words for what to do when they need to engage the skill of problem solving. If the child can come up with a more significant mnemonic – even better!

Right here, right now!

It is good to help the child understand that we can't change the past, but we can learn from it. Explain that we can plan for the future but we can't do anything about it until it arrives so there is no point in worrying about it too much! Living in the here and now, being the best that we can be and appreciating what we have, is the ideal way to handle stress and anxiety.

Technique 16 – Mindfulness

Mindfulness has become very popular in the past few years. It is a valuable technique used to reduce stress and anxiety. Even without stress and anxiety, mindfulness is a very simple, yet effective, practice that can enhance anyone's day-to-day living. Practising mindfulness can bring about better sleep, a calmer self and ultimately a positive change in anyone's life.

To explain it in very basic terms, mindfulness is the act of living in the moment, without judgment or trying to change it. It is about simply experiencing the here and now rather than spending our time constantly worrying about the past or future.

This particular technique is a mindfulness meditation and very relaxing for the child. However, being mindful can happen anywhere at any time, by just staying in the moment.

Technique 17 – Thankful time

Thankful Time is all about seeing the positives in our lives and not taking them for granted. It is good for children to recognise what positives surround them daily. It is even better for them to be grateful for them. Things to be thankful for can be the simplest of things that happened that day! For example, having dinner, riding a bike around, enjoying the sunny weather ….

Depression is an illness that robs us of our ability to see the positives in life. It is like a black cloud that darkens even the brightest of days. In cases where the child may be suffering with this, it is important to be patient. It may be obvious to us what is good in the child's life or what was good about their day but the illness can blind them to the positives. I would definitely recommend that even in times like this, Thankful Time is carried out at night. It may be a difficult task and seem meaningless but the act of being thankful for the positives in our lives, night after night, will eventually have a positive effect.

Sometimes my child worries ... what do I do?

Again, this can be done anywhere at any time. However, this particular technique works well as part of a routine i.e. at roughly the same time every day e.g. just before bed. It can be a verbal action or a written one depending on what the child prefers. However, the act of writing them down reaffirms them and the child then has a 'thankful' record to look back on.

Note from the Author

My background is in secondary school education teaching Geography and Business. I took a career break when my second child was born then decided to stay at home full-time to care for them.

I hold a Diploma and Advanced Diploma in Hypnotherapy and Psychotherapy from the Institute of Clinical Hypnotherapy and Psychotherapy Ireland. I also have a practitioner's Certificate in Cognitive Behavioural Therapy and Neuro Linguistic Programming practitioner training. During my career break I wrote a women's fictional novel, *To Have, Not Hold!* I love writing and find it is an effective way to manage my own anxiety.

I have always had an interest in adolescent mental health which lead me to be a teacher. I developed an interest in the mental well-being of younger children when my own children were born and I realised how prevalent the issue of anxiety is.

I suffered with mental health issues as a teenager and my eldest daughter had quite bad anxiety. With the techniques and knowledge that I gained from my own experiences and through my studies, I was able to help her significantly reduce her anxiety to a manageable level.

Sometimes my child worries … what do I do?

I decided to write the children's book and course because the numbers of children suffering anxiety were growing exponentially and I felt there were no age-appropriate resources available to help them. Patients with low-level anxiety are on long waiting lists for mental health services that were initially set up to deal with moderate to severe mental health issues.

I believe this low-level anxiety is manageable and with a little knowledge and the right set of therapeutic techniques, it can be managed within the home. I also believe that we really do need to tackle child anxiety because if it is not managed now, we will be facing further serious mental health issues in the future. If we are not equipped to deal with the issues now, what will it be like in ten, twenty years?

I would love to see something in place in primary education to ensure children's mental health is being cared for just as their physical well-being is with healthy lunch policies, vaccines, dental check-ups, etc. I feel mental well-being needs to become a priority *now*. Taking that into consideration, this book and the children's book *Sometimes I worry … how about you?* are a simple way the parent, guardian or teacher can approach children's anxiety in the home or in an educational setting. I am by no means saying they are the solution to this epidemic, but they can be a useful aid and a practical resource. And that has to be a good place to start!

NOTES

NOTES